SCHOOL STRIKE for CLIMATE

BY NEL YOMTOV
ILLUSTRATED BY FERN CANO

CONSULTANT:
SANYA CARLEY, PhD
PROFESSOR, O'NEILL SCHOOL OF PUBLIC AND
ENVIRONMENTAL AFFAIRS
INDIANA UNIVERSITY

CAPSTONE PRESS
a capstone imprint

Published by Capstone Press, an imprint of Capstone.
1710 Roe Crest Drive, North Mankato, Minnesota 56003
capstonepub.com

Library of Congress Cataloging-in-Publication Data
Names: Yomtov, Nelson, author. I Cano, Fernando, illustrator.
Title: School strike for climate / by Nel Yomtov ; illustrated by Fern Cano.
Description: North Mankato, Minnesota : Capstone Press, [2022] I Series: Movements and resistance I Includes bibliographical references. I Audience: Ages 8-11 I Audience: Grades 4-6 I
Summary: "In August 2018, a teenager named Greta Thunberg missed school to sit outside the Swedish parliament with a sign that read School Strike for Climate. She was demanding that government leaders take stronger action against climate change due to global warming. At first, Greta sat alone. But her message spread. Other students joined her in the movement that became known as Fridays for Future. By September 2019, millions of activists from around the world marched in protests to protect the future of the planet"--Provided by publisher.
Identifiers: LCCN 2021033230 (print) I LCCN 2021033231 (ebook) I ISBN 9781663959232 (hardcover) I ISBN 9781666324396 (paperback) I ISBN 9781666324389 (pdf) I ISBN 9781666324358 (kindle edition)
Subjects: LCSH: Climatic changes--Prevention--Citizen participation--Comic books, strips, etc. I Student strikes--Comic books, strips, etc. I Thunberg, Greta, 2003---Comic books, strips, etc. I LCGFT: Nonfiction comics. I Graphic novels.
Classification: LCC QC903.15 .Y66 2022 (print) I LCC QC903.15 (ebook) I DDC 363.738/747--dc23
LC record available at https://lccn.loc.gov/2021033230
LC ebook record available at https://lccn.loc.gov/2021033231

Editorial Credits
Editor: Kristen Mohn; Designer: Tracy Davies;
Media Researcher: Svetlana Zhurkin; Production Specialist: Katy LaVigne

TABLE OF CONTENTS

THE SCIENCE IS SETTLED............................4

A GIRL NAMED GRETA..............................8

THE GLOBAL WEEK FOR FUTURE 16

PRAISE, CRITICISM, AND PROGRESS.....24

MORE ABOUT THE CLIMATE STRIKES 28

GLOSSARY 30

READ MORE 31

INTERNET SITES..31

ABOUT THE AUTHOR...............................32

ABOUT THE ILLUSTRATOR........................32

THE SCIENCE IS SETTLED

By the late 20th century, the evidence was clear. Earth was in trouble—big trouble.

Studies showed that 97 percent of climate scientists agreed. Climate change was real—and it was extremely likely due to human activities.

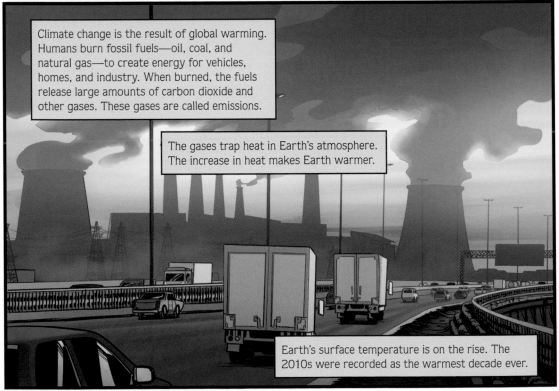

Climate change is the result of global warming. Humans burn fossil fuels—oil, coal, and natural gas—to create energy for vehicles, homes, and industry. When burned, the fuels release large amounts of carbon dioxide and other gases. These gases are called emissions.

The gases trap heat in Earth's atmosphere. The increase in heat makes Earth warmer.

Earth's surface temperature is on the rise. The 2010s were recorded as the warmest decade ever.

Hotter temperatures cause the climate to change. Ice caps in Greenland, Antarctica, and the Arctic are melting at alarming rates. The habitats of polar bears and other animals are disappearing.

The melting ice leads to rising sea levels, which can cause deadly floods.

Climate change also causes other extreme weather events, such as hurricanes, heat waves, and droughts.

Food production may be affected, leading to hunger in some parts of the world. Flooded communities may not have access to clean water.

Millions of people have already been forced to leave their lands due to the effects of climate change.

In December 2015, nearly 200 countries, including the United States, signed the Paris Agreement.

This treaty on climate set a goal of limiting long-term global warming to less than 3.6 degrees Fahrenheit (2 degrees Celsius). Scientists warned an increase of any more could be devastating.

To achieve the goal, countries that signed this agreement pledged to reduce their carbon emissions.

In 2017, President Donald Trump announced he was pulling the United States out of the agreement.

For Americans the Paris Agreement means lost jobs, lower wages, shuttered factories, and lower economic production.

No other countries pulled out of the agreement. The countries that remained were still honoring their pledge.

In 2018, Hoesung Lee, the chief of the Intergovernmental Panel on Climate Change (IPCC) presented a report to the United Nations. The IPCC provides scientific climate data to policy makers.

Reducing carbon emissions can create a safer, healthier, and more prosperous society.

The report found that meeting the Paris Agreement's goal of limiting global warming would require "rapid, far-reaching and unprecedented changes."

If the goal wasn't met, Earth risked rising sea levels, food shortages, deadly heat, and superstorms.

Global warming deeply concerned a young Swedish girl named Greta Thunberg.

Without treating this as a real crisis, we cannot solve it.

It's about us and our future and future generations.

A GIRL NAMED GRETA

Greta Thunberg was born on January 3, 2003, in Stockholm, Sweden. Her mother, Malena Ernman, is an opera singer. Her father, Svante Thunberg, is an actor.

Thunberg was eight years old when she first heard about climate change.

Floods are just one of the dangerous effects of climate change. Destructive storms and droughts are already happening.

The future of millions of kids like me is in serious danger.

Thunberg was very worried. But there was something deeper going on.

At 11, she became ill with depression. She stopped speaking, and she stopped going to school. She ate very little.

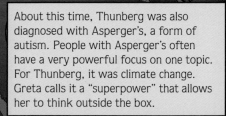

About this time, Thunberg was also diagnosed with Asperger's, a form of autism. People with Asperger's often have a very powerful focus on one topic. For Thunberg, it was climate change. Greta calls it a "superpower" that allows her to think outside the box.

Greta continued to learn about climate change. Gaining knowledge helped heal her depression. She began eating more, and she returned to school. She taught her parents about the dangers of climate change. Greta began to think she could make a difference.

Something has to be done.

In May 2018, Thunberg wrote an essay about climate change that was printed in a Swedish newspaper. After speaking with other young climate activists, she suggested school strikes.

When other activists decided against the idea, Thunberg decided to strike alone. Her hope was to pressure the Swedish government into meeting the goals of the Paris Agreement.

On August 20, 2018, Thunberg skipped school. She headed to the Swedish parliament with a sign reading "School Strike for Climate" in Swedish.

Thunberg passed out flyers with facts about the effects of climate change.

Shouldn't you be in school?

I am school striking for climate. Since you adults don't care about my future, I won't either.

By early September, other young people had joined Thunberg's climate strike. She announced she would strike every Friday until Sweden acted quicker to reduce carbon emissions.

The Fridays for Future movement was born.

Thunberg tweeted about her strike. Climate activists retweeted her posts to thousands of people around the world. Thunberg's message spread like wildfire.

On October 20, 2018, she addressed a crowd of 10,000 people in Helsinki, Finland. She meant for her words to be heard by world leaders.

This is a cry for help.

The future of all coming generations rests on your shoulders. So please treat the crisis as the crisis it is and give us a future. Our lives are in your hands.

Within a few weeks, students from other countries were striking. They used #FridaysForFuture to spread their cause.

Leah Namugerwa helped start a chapter of Fridays for Future in Uganda. Young strikers there demanded "Climate Justice" and warned that "Earth Is on Fire." Severe droughts and flooding due to climate change have killed many people in the country.

SAVE THE PLANET

FRIDAYS FOR FUTURE

Thunberg's efforts motivated people of all ages. Among her millions of followers were a group of older Swedish activists who called themselves "Greta's Oldies."

It's been inspirational for me to walk in Greta's footsteps.

GRETA'S GAMLINGAR

In December 2018, Thunberg addressed world leaders at the United Nations Climate Change Conference in Poland. Greta's words were harsh, but sincere.

If a few children can get headlines all over the world just by not going to school, then imagine what we could all do together if we really wanted to.

You say you love your children above all else. Yet you are stealing their future in front of their very eyes.

We have come here to let you know that change is coming . . .

. . . whether you like it or not.

Thunberg continued to speak with world leaders and corporations to highlight the threat of global warming.

She traveled from country to country by train and by boat. She did not fly because of the carbon emissions of jet planes.

In January 2019, Thunberg addressed political and economic leaders at a convention in Switzerland.

I don't want your hope. I want you to panic. I want you to feel the fear I feel every day.

And then I want you to act. I want you to act as if the house was on fire.

Because it is.

Thunberg's activism had inspired a worldwide movement.

Young people were ready to take their cause to the streets.

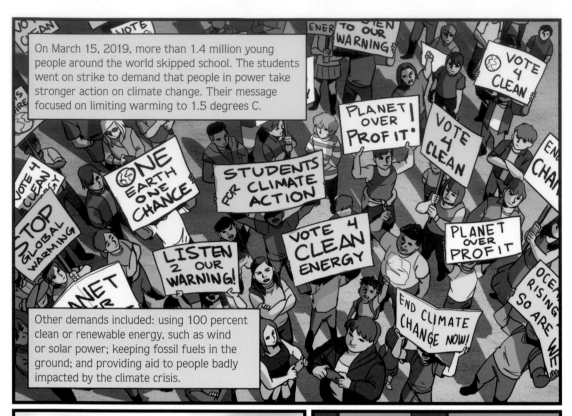

On March 15, 2019, more than 1.4 million young people around the world skipped school. The students went on strike to demand that people in power take stronger action on climate change. Their message focused on limiting warming to 1.5 degrees C.

Other demands included: using 100 percent clean or renewable energy, such as wind or solar power; keeping fossil fuels in the ground; and providing aid to people badly impacted by the climate crisis.

The event took place in more than 2,000 cities and towns in at least 125 countries.

315 청소년 기후 행동 GLOBAL CLIMATE STRIKE FOR FUTURE

In subzero temperatures, scientists in Antarctica came out to support the students.

The young protestors were deeply concerned about climate change and its future effects.

"It is the biggest threat in human history," said the group that organized the global strike. "And we will not accept the world's decision-makers' inaction that threatens our entire civilization."

The strikers were putting the heat on world leaders to act—and to act quickly.

A second global school strike was held in May 2019. More than 1 million people marched in about 125 countries. Thunberg led marchers in her hometown of Stockholm.

Yet the biggest strike was still to come.

THE GLOBAL WEEK FOR FUTURE

In late May 2019, Thunberg and an international group of climate activists wrote an invitation announcing new strikes.

The invitation declared, "Starting on Friday, September 20, we will kick start a week of climate action with worldwide strikes. . . . We must act."

All around the world, millions of children and adults saw the invitation online.

The strikes would take place in September, around the time of two important meetings at the United Nations in New York City.

In the United States, youth-led climate activist groups helped organize the strikes and get the word out. They included the US Youth Climate Strike Coalition, Earth Guardians, Zero Hour, and Future Coalition.

Katie Eder, founder of Future Coalition, was one of the strike's most active supporters.

Young people are uniting around September 20 in a way we've never seen before! This is a fight for our futures, and time is running out.

Thunberg and her organizers' hard work was paying off.

As the strikes neared, Greta kept busy. On September 17, she appeared before a congressional hearing in Washington, D.C.

I have not come to offer any prepared remarks at this hearing. I am instead attaching my testimony. It is the IPCC Special Report on Global Warming.

I don't want you to listen to me. I want you to listen to the scientists.

And I want you to unite behind the science.

Then I want you to take real action.

Greta's big week was just beginning.

On September 20, the global climate strike became the largest mass protest on global warming in history.

Seventeen strikes were reported in the Philippines.

In New York City, a 17-year-old girl named Xiye Bastida was one of the leaders of the protests.

In Zagreb, Croatia . . .

. . . Paris, France . . .

. . . the Solomon Islands in the South Pacific . . .

The science has been crystal clear. How dare you continue to look away and come here saying that you're doing enough?

You are failing us. And if you choose to fail us, I say: We will never forgive you.

The world is waking up. And change is coming, whether you like it or not.

Greta and her fellow climate activists had taken the world by storm.

PRAISE, CRITICISM, AND PROGRESS

The shock waves created by the school strikes for climate were felt around the world. Many people supported the young activists. In England, a group of scientists and professors praised the strikes . . .

We are inspired that our children, spurred on by the noble actions of Greta Thunberg . . . are making their voices heard.

. . . as did U.N. Secretary-General António Guterres . . .

These schoolchildren have grasped something that seems to elude many of their elders: We are in a race for our lives, and we are losing.

But not everyone was convinced the strikers were right. Some people criticized the students for skipping school. Others, such as climate scientist Judith Curry, questioned their claims.

Climate strikers refer to climate change as a life-and-death crisis. This is nonsense.

And some went so far as to criticize Thunberg personally by calling her cruel names.

PERSON of the YEAR
TIME
GRETA THUNBERG
THE POWER OF YOUTH

Even President Donald Trump mocked Thunberg after she was named TIME magazine's 2019 Person of the Year.

He claimed TIME's selection of her was "ridiculous" and said Thunberg should learn to control her anger.

Regardless of the praise or criticism, the school strikes have led to progress. The sheer size and international reach of the strikes have focused public attention on the climate crisis.

Online coverage, newspapers, television, and social media have spread the word to hundreds of millions of people around the globe.

The strikes helped shift public opinion. A poll conducted in 2018 showed that 46 percent of American adults believed that dealing with climate change should be a top priority.

By 2020, the number jumped to 52 percent.

%US Adults Who Say Dealing With Climate Change Should Be A Top Priority For The President And Congress

52%

30%

2008 2010 2012 2014 2016 2018 2020

The strikes also forced politicians to take climate change seriously. In 2020, German Chancellor Angela Merkel met with Thunberg and acknowledged her influence.

We want people to step up . . . to prioritize the future . . . and to be brave enough to think long-term.

On the global level, however, there has been little progress actually reducing carbon emissions since the strikes began.

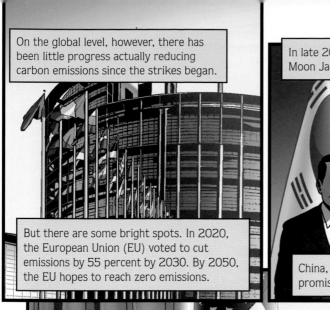

But there are some bright spots. In 2020, the European Union (EU) voted to cut emissions by 55 percent by 2030. By 2050, the EU hopes to reach zero emissions.

In late 2020, South Korean President Moon Jae-in also pledged action.

We will actively aim for zero emissions by 2050.

China, the largest producer of global emissions, promised to reach zero emissions by 2060.

Immediately upon taking office in January 2021, newly elected president Joe Biden signed an order for the United States to reenter the Paris Agreement.

We can no longer delay or do the bare minimum to address climate change.

Time will tell if the school strikes for climate help save our planet. But Earth's future looks a little brighter when young activists around the world spread their good ideas.

MORE ABOUT THE CLIMATE STRIKES

- Renewable energy is power made from resources that nature will replace. Wind, water, and sunlight are forms of renewable energy. Renewable energy is also called "clean energy" or "green power" because it doesn't pollute the environment.

- The Intergovernmental Panel on Climate Change (IPCC) is an organization made up of scientists and economists from around the world. The group was formed by the United Nations in 1988. The IPCC produces reports that contribute to the world's understanding of climate change and its global political and economic impacts.

- In 2018, Katie Eder, the executive director of Future Coalition, organized 50 Miles More, a group working to address global warming, gun violence, and racism in the United States.

- In 2020, the coronavirus limited participation in the climate strikes. Despite social distancing and other COVID-19 restrictions, many activists around the world took to the streets and social media to keep their message alive.

- Atlas Sarrafoglu, the leader of the September 2019 strikes in Turkey, was awarded a 2020 World Wide Fund for Nature Youth Award for his work as a climate activist.

- On September 25, 2020, Greta Thunberg led a socially distanced strike in Sweden. Only 50 people participated due to the country's lockdown laws. "So we adapt," Greta tweeted. "School strike week 110," she wrote.

- The ongoing COVID-19 pandemic failed to dampen the spirit of climate strikers in 2021. Climate strikes took place in more than 50 countries in March.

- Thousands of students in Australia walked out of their classrooms to participate in school strikes for climate in May 2021. Strikes took place in about 50 places, including the major cities of Brisbane, Melbourne, and Sydney. Hundreds of businesses around the country closed to support the students' action. Organizers worked with local health authorities to make sure participants followed coronavirus safety guidelines in their region.

- Also in May 2021, President Joe Biden announced plans to launch a large-scale government program, the Civilian Climate Corps (CCC), which would employ young people to work on lessening the impact of climate change. The program would create well-paying jobs for teens and 20-somethings with the added goal of launching corps members into environmental careers. Preserving wetlands and other wildlife habitats, fighting wildfires, organizing food programs, and promoting local climate policies are among the many types of jobs the CCC will offer.

GLOSSARY

activist (AK-tiv-ist)—a person who works to bring about political or social change

autism (AW-tiz-uhm)—a condition that causes someone to have difficulties learning, communicating, or forming relationships with people

crisis (CRY-sis)—a time of severe difficulty or danger

depression (dih-PREH-shuhn)—an emotional disorder that causes people to feel sad and tired

drought (DROWT)—a long period without rain

elude (eh-LOOD)—to escape or get away

emissions (eh-MISH-uhnz)—substances released into the atmosphere

fossil fuels (FAH-sil FYOO-uhlz)—coal, oil, or natural gas

heat wave (HEET WAYV)—a period of unusually hot weather

hurricane (HUR-uh-kane)—a very large storm with high winds and rain; hurricanes form over warm ocean water

mock (MAHK)—to tease or laugh at someone in a mean way

prosperous (PROSS-pur-uhs)—bringing wealth and success

renewable energy (rih-NOO-uh-buhl EN-ur-jee)—power from sources that can never be used up, such as wind and sunlight

strike (STRIKE)—a situation in which workers or students refuse to work or go to school until their demands are met

treaty (TREE-tee)—a formal agreement between nations related to peace, alliance, or trade

READ MORE

Harman, Alice. *Climate Change and How We'll Fix It: The Real Problem and What We Can Do to Fix It.* New York: Sterling Children's Books, 2021.

Part, Michael. *The Greta Thunberg Story: Being Different Is a Superpower.* Beverly Hills, CA: Sole Books, 2019.

Simon, Seymour. *Climate Action: What Happened and What We Can Do.* New York: HarperCollins, 2021.

INTERNET SITES

Greta Thunberg: Greta Thunberg: Who is the climate campaigner and what are her aims?
bbc.com/news/world-europe-49918719

School Strike for Climate!
natgeokids.com/za/kids-club/cool-kids/from-you/school-strikes-for-climate/

What Is Climate Change?
climatekids.nasa.gov/climate-change-meaning/

ABOUT THE AUTHOR

Nel Yomtov is a writer of children's nonfiction books and graphic novels. He specializes in writing about history, science, and biography. Nel has written several graphic novels for Capstone. His graphic novel adaptation, *Jason and the Golden Fleece*, published by Stone Arch Books/Capstone was a winner of the 2009 Moonbeam Children's Book Award and the 2011 Lighthouse Literature Award. Nel lives in the New York City area.

ABOUT THE ILLUSTRATOR

Fern Cano is an emerging illustrator born in Mexico City, Mexico. He currently resides in Monterrey, Mexico, where he works as a full-time illustrator and colorist at Graphikslava studio. He has done illustration work for Marvel, DC Comics, and role-playing games like *Pathfinder* from Paizo Publishing. In his spare time, he enjoys hanging out with friends, singing, rowing, and drawing.